BASEBALL LEGENDS

Hank Aaron
Grover Cleveland Alexander
Ernie Banks
Johnny Bench
Yogi Berra
Roy Campanella
Roberto Clemente
Ty Cobb
Dizzy Dean
Joe DiMaggio
Bob Feller
Jimmie Foxx
Lou Gehrig
Bob Gibson
Rogers Hornsby
Reggie Jackson
Shoeless Joe Jackson
Walter Johnson
Sandy Koufax
Mickey Mantle
Christy Mathewson
Willie Mays
Stan Musial
Satchel Paige
Brooks Robinson
Frank Robinson
Jackie Robinson
Pete Rose
Babe Ruth
Nolan Ryan
Mike Schmidt
Tom Seaver
Duke Snider
Warren Spahn
Willie Stargell
Casey Stengel
Honus Wagner
Ted Williams
Carl Yastrzemski
Cy Young

NEWFIELD
PUBLICATIONS

BASEBALL LEGENDS

SHOELESS JOE JACKSON

Jack Kavanagh

Introduction by
Jim Murray

Senior Consultant
Earl Weaver

CHELSEA HOUSE PUBLISHERS
New York • Philadelphia

Published by arrangement
with Chelsea House Publishers.
Newfield Publications and design
are federally registered trademarks
of Newfield Publications, Inc.

CHELSEA HOUSE PUBLISHERS

Editorial Director: Richard Rennert
Executive Managing Editor: Karyn Gullen Browne
Copy Chief: Robin James
Picture Editor: Adrian G. Allen
Art Director: Robert Mitchell
Manufacturing Director: Gerald Levine

Baseball Legends
Senior Editor: Philip Koslow

Staff for SHOELESS JOE JACKSON
Copy Editor: Catherine Iannone
Editorial Assistant: Scott Briggs
Designer: M. Cambraia Magalhães
Picture Researcher: Alan Gottlieb
Cover Illustration: Daniel O'Leary

Library of Congress Cataloging-in-Publication Data

Kavanagh, Jack.
Shoeless Joe Jackson / Jack Kavanagh.;
    p. cm.—(Baseball legends)
    Includes bibliographical references and index.
    ISBN 0–7910–2170–X (hc)
    1. Jackson, Joe, 1888–1951— Juvenile literature. 2. Baseball
players—United States—Biography—Juvenile literature. 3. Chicago
White Sox (Baseball team)—Juvenile literature. 4. Baseball
players. [1.Jackson, Joe, 1888–1951.]   I. Title.   II. Series.
GV865.J29K38 1995   94–21264
796.357'092 dc20   CIP
[B]   AC

CONTENTS

WHAT MAKES A STAR

Jim Murray

No one has ever been able to explain to me the mysterious alchemy that makes one man a .350 hitter and another player, more or less identical in physical makeup, hard put to hit .200. You look at an Al Kaline, who played with the Detroit Tigers from 1953 to 1974. He was pale, stringy, almost poetic-looking. He always seemed to be struggling against a bad case of mononucleosis. But with a bat in his hands, he was King Kong. During his career, he hit 399 home runs, rapped out 3,007 hits, and compiled a .297 batting average.

Form isn't the reason. The first time anybody saw Roberto Clemente step into the batter's box for the Pittsburgh Pirates, the best guess was that Clemente would be back in Double A ball in a week. He had one foot in the bucket and held his bat at an awkward angle—he looked as though he couldn't hit an outside pitch. A lot of other ballplayers may have had a better-looking stance. Yet they never led the National League in hitting in four different years, the way Clemente did.

Not every ballplayer is born with the ability to hit a curveball. Nor is exceptional hand-eye coordination the key to heavy hitting. Big-league locker rooms are filled with players who have all the attributes, save one: discipline. Every baseball man can tell you a story about a pitcher who throws a ball faster than anyone has ever seen but who has no control on or *off* the field.

The Hall of Fame is full of people who transformed themselves into great ballplayers by working at the sport, by studying the game, and making sacrifices. They're overachievers—and winners. If you want to find them, just watch the World Series. Or simply read about New York Yankee great Lou Gehrig; Ted Williams, "the Splendid Splinter" of the Boston Red Sox; or the Dodgers' strikeout king Sandy Koufax.

A pitcher *should* be able to win a lot of ballgames with a 98-miles-per-hour fastball. But what about the pitcher who wins 20 games a year with a fastball so slow that you can catch it with your teeth? Bob Feller of the Cleveland Indians got into the Hall of Fame with a blazing fastball that glowed in the dark. National League star Grover Cleveland Alexander got there with a pitch that took considerably longer to reach the plate; but when it did arrive, the pitch was exactly where Alexander wanted it to be—and the last place the batter expected it to be.

There are probably more players with exceptional ability who didn't make it to the major leagues than there are who did. A number of great hitters, bored with fielding practice, had to be dropped from their team because their home-run production didn't make up for their lapses in the field. And then there are players like Brooks Robinson of the Baltimore Orioles, who made himself into a human vacuum cleaner at third base because he knew that working hard to become an expert fielder would win him a job in the big leagues.

A star is not something that flashes through the sky. That's a comet. Or a meteor. A star is something you can steer ships by. It stays in place and gives off a steady glow; it is fixed, permanent. A star works at being a star.

And that's how you tell a star in baseball. He shows up night after night and takes pride in how brightly he shines. He's Willie Mays running so hard his hat keeps falling off; Ty Cobb sliding to stretch a single into a double; Lou Gehrig, after being fooled in his first two at-bats, belting the next pitch off the light tower because he's taken the time to study the pitcher. Stars never take themselves for granted. That's why they're stars.

1

"SAY IT AIN'T SO, JOE!"

It was a Saturday afternoon in Chicago when Joe Jackson, known to everyone as Shoeless Joe, stepped up to bat in Comiskey Park in the midst of a tight American League pennant race between the hometown White Sox and the Cleveland Indians. The year was 1920, one of the most exciting in baseball history. Attendance figures had been shattered during the season as fans packed into stadiums everywhere to see the titans of baseball, such as Jackson and Ty Cobb, do battle. At the beginning of the year, the New York Yankees had paid the unheard-of sum of $125,000 to the Boston Red Sox for a 25-year-old player named Babe Ruth, who promptly rewarded the team by crashing an almost unbelievable total of 54 home runs (the runner-up, George Sisler of the St. Louis Browns, hit 19, and the highest total for any other *team* in the major leagues was 50). But Jackson's team, the Chicago White Sox, was generally considered the greatest of its day, and Shoeless Joe was the Chisox' star.

As the pitch came over the plate Jackson unleashed Black Betsy, the famous bat that he had carefully carved and stained himself. He

Shoeless Joe Jackson and Happy Felsch, star outfielders of the 1919 Chicago White Sox, pose for photographers during the 1917 World Series. Three years later, the two players were enmeshed in the greatest scandal in baseball history.

drove the ball deep over the right-field fence and raced around the bases as the Chicagoans roared with glee. No baseball fans were more loyal nor more knowledgeable about the game than the citizens of Chicago's South Side—and Jackson was their man. Jackson sparked his team to a 5–1 win that day, and at the end of the season his batting average stood at a lofty .382. He led the league in triples with 20, scored 105 runs, and drove in 121. Jackson had clearly had his best year since joining the White Sox in 1916.

But Jackson's life in the fall of 1920 was more complicated than the gaudy stats and adoring fans suggested. Gambling had become a major pastime in America, especially at the beginning of the wild 1920s, and for years there had been rumors that gamblers and ballplayers had conspired together to fix baseball games. Now suspicion had fallen on the White Sox: rumor had it that some of the team's players had thrown the 1919 World Series, purposely losing to the Cincinnati Reds. A grand jury had convened in Chicago to investigate charges that a 1920 game had been fixed, and the jury had been told that it might want to examine the allegations about the Series. The more time passed, the more the rumors spread.

The next day Jackson played again in Comiskey Park, and by the day's end the Sox had easily beaten the Detroit Tigers. The victory lifted the Sox into first place, but strangely the fans did not seem elated. Since the previous day's game, the talk of a World Series fix involving several White Sox players—including the great Jackson—had come out into the open. Gloom seemed to hang over the Chicago crowd, even as they loyally applauded the Sox players, including those accused of being in on the fix.

On this muggy day when no sun shone, more than 200 fans, mostly young boys, followed Joe Jackson and outfielder Happy Felsch as they left Comiskey Park. Nineteen-year-old James T. Farrell, later a best-selling novelist, was among the crowd. Years later he recalled the scene: "A few fans called to [Jackson and Felsch], but they gave no acknowledgment to these greetings. They turned and started to walk away. Spontaneously, the crowd followed in a slow, disorderly manner. I went with the crowd and trailed about five feet behind Jackson and Felsch. They walked somewhat slowly. A fan called out: 'It ain't true, Joe.' The two suspected players did not turn back. They walked on slowly. The crowd took up the cry and more than once men and boys called out and repeated: 'It ain't true, Joe.' This call followed Jackson and Felsch as they walked all the way under the stands."

Over the years, this scene was gradually enshrined in American folklore. As with most legends, the story has been modified in the retelling. The most popular version, found in many reference books and collections of baseball anecdotes, has a small boy coming up to Jackson and tugging on the player's sleeve. When Jackson looks down, the young fan tearfully pleads, "Say it ain't so, Joe." Although this catchy phrase has been repeated countless times, Farrell's account of the event has the ring of historical truth.

The following day, the White Sox beat Detroit 2–0 in their final home game. Jackson's base hit that day had helped win the game, but when he reached the locker room he found a stack of

Chicago papers echoing the headline the Philadelphia *North American* had blazoned across its morning edition: THE MOST GIGANTIC SPORTING SWINDLE IN THE HISTORY OF AMERICA! Billy Maharg, a former baseball player, had told a reporter that he had helped fix the 1919 World Series. Jackson, who was illiterate, could not read the papers, but one look at his teammates' faces told him what was happening. He knew that from this point on his life was going to be radically different. The next day he was called to testify before the grand jury, and he told them all he knew.

Jackson and seven of his teammates soon received a telegram from club owner Charles Comiskey notifying them that they were suspended from the White Sox until they were either cleared of the charges or found guilty. It would be a long 10 months before the eight ballplayers—now derided as the Chicago Black Sox—actually stood trial.

A tense-looking Jackson (right) confers with Illinois assistant state attorney Harley Replogle in September 1920. Jackson had just told a Chicago grand jury about the scheme to fix the 1919 World Series; while admitting that he had accepted a $5,000 bribe, he maintained that he had played to win.

The accusations were a terrible blow to baseball fans. At the century's beginning, when a mood of cheerful optimism prevailed in America, people found it hard to believe that the national pastime could be corrupt. It was hardest of all to believe that someone like Joe Jackson could be in any way involved: the great athlete did not even have to pretend to be a simple soul, for everyone realized at once that he was. It was common knowledge that Jackson was unable to read.

His down-home style had earned him the nickname Shoeless Joe. As a teenage semipro player, he once shucked off a new pair of shoes that had blistered his feet, and played a game in his socks.

Yet this unassuming man was also called the greatest natural hitter who ever played the game of baseball. Babe Ruth copied his batting stance, and Ty Cobb considered Jackson the finest left fielder he had ever seen. It was difficult for anyone to understand how an athlete as great as Joe Jackson, a man so sincere, could be involved in any kind of corruption.

To this day people dispute the issue of Jackson's involvement in the 1919 World Series scandal and his right to be in the Baseball Hall of Fame. But there are two things that baseball enthusiasts and historians generally agree on: that Jackson was one of the greatest ballplayers of all time and that he is the game's most tragic figure. Like many complex stories, this one has simple beginnings. For Jackson, the story begins in the piney backcountry of South Carolina.

2

"HE MUST BE SOME WHALE"

oseph Jefferson Jackson was born on a run-down plantation in Pickens County, South Carolina, on July 16, 1887. Life on the plantation was exceedingly hard, for its owner was a strange and fiery old man who mistreated his tenants. George Jackson, young Joe's father, barely managed to scrape together a living by sharecropping the poor, rocky soil. The environment that Joe knew as a child was so harsh that if a man learned to read or write, he was regarded as a freak.

Eventually textile mills began to move down from the North, looking for cheap labor. Mill work became the region's biggest source of jobs and gave Joe's father a chance to break free from life on the plantation. When Joe was six years old, the Jacksons moved to Brandon Mill, a small cotton mill town near Greenville, in the northwest corner of South Carolina, in the foothills of the Blue Ridge Mountains. Like other families who worked for the textile mill, the Jacksons occupied a small wood-frame row house in a company-owned village.

The workroom of a South Carolina textile mill, photographed around 1910. When young Joe Jackson went to work in the mills at the age of six, he faced a lifetime of hard and dangerous toil; but his baseball talent soon offered a way out.

Joe's family still lived in rural poverty, but Joe's youth was hardly the life of a Huckleberry Finn. When Joe was only six years old, he had to put on an older brother's hand-me-down work shoes and join his father, six brothers, and two sisters in working at the Brandon Cotton Mill. The thundering looms were unguarded, and the machinery made a frightening noise.

Many of the Jacksons' neighbors lost arms, legs, or even their lives working in the mills. One day, Joe's brother Davey was caught in the machinery and carried right off his feet. When he was thrown clear, he was maimed for life. Joe himself could have easily been mangled as many mill workers were. But despite the dangers of mill work, Joe's father told him that it was much better than the plantation had been.

The Brandon Cotton Mill may have given the Jacksons their livelihood, but it took away their independence. The millworkers drew small pay-checks and spent most of their wages to buy groceries at the company-owned store. Because they often needed credit to keep food on the table, families such as the Jacksons often found themselves indebted to the company for life. There was little chance of moving to a better-paying job or of owning their own home. But just as the mill job had allowed Joe's father to escape from the plantation, so Joe Jackson would use baseball to escape from the dangerous and impoverished life of a mill worker.

All the mills promoted their own baseball teams, and Brandon Mill was no exception. Mill workers who played on the company team were given easy jobs during the week and time off to practice, and they were paid to play Saturday games against other local teams. Large for his age and gifted with an uncanny coordination, Joe won a place on the mill's baseball squad in 1901, when he was only 13.

When Joe reported to his team, he brought his own bat with him. He had carved the bat by hand from a tight-grained piece of timber. After staining and hand-rubbing it to an ebony luster, Joe named the bat Black Betsy. It became a good-luck charm that he could put to work hitting screaming line drives. All his baseball life, Joe Jackson looked for wood that could be turned into replicas of his original Black Betsy. The bat was 36 inches long and weighed about 48 ounces, far longer and heavier than the bats used by modern-day ballplayers.

Jackson always jealously guarded his bat, but other players kept clear of it anyway, mainly because they could not swing it with the ease that he did. The thick handle was just right for his huge hands. With his powerful physique, Jackson could whip Black Betsy through the strike zone and send a baseball great distances.

Joe Jackson is regarded to have had the best swing in baseball history. Babe Ruth, who had been a great left-handed pitcher before he switched to the outfield, adopted Jackson's swing when he became a full-time hitter. "Why not?" the Babe remarked years later, "Joe had the most perfect swing I ever saw." Ruth imitated Jackson's stance, holding his feet close together and taking a long stride into the ball. Ruth's clouts had a little more lift to them than Joe's trademark "blue darters," but basically both men hit the same way.

Unusually tall for a boy barely into his teens, Joe found himself playing ball with grown men on the mill teams. Despite his talent, he had

Jackson (fifth from left) joined the Greenville team of the Carolina Association in 1908 and led the league with a .346 average. His standout play drew the attention of the Phila- delphia Athletics, who brought him up to the majors at the end of the season.

some rough moments. He began as a catcher, and one of the team's pitchers, a burly mill hand, threw a fastball at him so hard that Joe could not stop it. The force of the pitch drove Joe's glove back into his mask with such force that the metal bar cut into his forehead, leaving a scar that he would carry for the rest of his life.

Because of his strong throwing arm, the team shifted Joe to the pitcher's mound. But he also proved a danger to his teammates, throwing one pitch so hard that it broke the catcher's arm. When the catcher quit in protest, Joe tried playing the outfield.

Even among seasoned ballplayers, young Joe's talents quickly stood out. In 1906 he was recruited by a Greenville semipro team, led by a former college star, Lollie Gray. The other players on the team were collegians and local players with solid credentials. Joe still seemed a boy among men.

But Joe continued to hold his own, and as he grew older, he began to attract the attention of established baseball people. In 1907, when Jackson was 19 years old, he was playing against a mill team whose second baseman was Tom Stouch, a onetime major leaguer. Stouch immediately recognized Jackson's amazing gifts. "This tall skinny-looking kid stepped up to the plate," Stouch later recalled. "He didn't appear to have much in him, but he drove the ball on a line to a spot where I was standing, like a bullet out of a gun. I thought to myself, if this rube hits 'em like that every time, he must be some whale. He was. He hit three times that game, twice for extra bases, and when he hit, he left a trail of blue flame behind them as they shot through the air."

When Stouch was hired as the manager of Greenville's team in a new league, the Carolina Association, he hired Jackson at $75 a month, almost twice the salary Jackson had been paid by the mill. Stouch had been recruiting players from around the state and moving them to Greenville. His best player just went on living at home and rode his bike to the ballpark.

3

THE RELUCTANT ROOKIE

Jackson's skills rapidly developed as he played daily against other professional ballplayers on the Greenville team. After the youngster had been in Greenville for only a month, word of his phenomenal ability spread. Connie Mack, the owner and manager of the Philadelphia Athletics, sent a scout to South Carolina to see Jackson play. After reading the scout's report, Mack bought Jackson's contract for $900, getting the bargain of his life.

Jackson completed his first year in professional baseball by hitting .346 for Greenville, leading the Carolina Association. It was something that he would do twice more: lead a league in hitting the first season he played in it.

The rookie outfielder had been told to report to the Athletics as soon as he finished the season at Greenville. Jackson, who had never been away from his family, began to have doubts about going to Philadelphia. He told Stouch, "I hardly know as how I'd like it in those big Northern cities."

Stouch tried to reassure the rookie, but Jackson stalled. He sensed that his backwoods ways would be out of place in a teeming, metropolitan

In 1910, the Athletics traded Jackson to Cleveland, where he quickly became a star. His .408 average in 1911 was the highest ever for a rookie.

environment. First, Jackson insisted that he had to play a benefit game with his former mill team before he could leave. He played the game and dazzled the hometown fans by smashing a home run far over the center-field fence. But once the benefit game was over, Jackson still put off reporting to Philadelphia. Mack fired off telegrams ordering Jackson to report, but Shoeless Joe sat tight.

Finally Mack asked Tom Stouch to escort the reluctant recruit north. Jackson and his former manager boarded the train together. Stouch even fed Jackson supper and put him in his berth, but when the train arrived in Philadelphia, Jackson was nowhere to be found. He had quietly slipped off the train at Charlotte, North Carolina, and caught the next train back to Greenville. From there he sent Mack a telegram that read, AM UNABLE TO COME TO PHILADELPHIA AT THIS TIME. JOE JACKSON.

Mack was thrown by his new star's conduct. The American League season was in its final weeks, and the Athletics owner was eager to see his new ballplayer in action. Mack turned to Socks Seybold, a veteran outfielder, and told him, "Go down to Greenville and get this fellow's brothers and sisters and whole family to come with you if necessary . . . but bring him back!"

Seybold delivered the unwilling rookie, and on his very first day in the North, Jackson played his first big league game. The date was August 25, 1908, and the fans had high expectations. Three thousand of them had come to Columbia Park on a cold, drizzly day to see the heralded rookie break in against the Cleveland

Naps, then nicknamed for their star second baseman, Napoleon Lajoie.

Heinie Berger, a veteran spitballer—the spitball was legal in the game until 1920—was Cleveland's pitcher. On a dark day his trick pitch was even harder to see. But Jackson's sharp eyes saw the ball dart toward him, and he laced a line drive to right field that was just foul. Jackson adjusted his stance, and on the next pitch he smashed a blue darter for a single to left. A runner scored, and Shoeless Joe had his first RBI. He made good contact three more times. In one at-bat, he drove the right fielder to the fence to pull down a ball that might have gone out if it had not been waterlogged by the constant rain.

Jackson swiftly demonstrated his other skills. He caught a long drive that was hit far over his head, running it down and then whirling to cut down a runner at the plate with a perfect one-bounce peg. On another play he short-hopped a line drive hit up the middle and threw a strike into the catcher's glove to nail another runner. In his first major league game, Jackson made Connie Mack's eyes light up.

The rain that had begun during the ballgame continued for several days. When it finally stopped, making it possible to play ball again, Jackson was already back in South Carolina. The veteran members of the ballclub had found out he was illiterate and had played tricks on the naive newcomer, knowing that he was too unsophisticated to defend himself. In those rough and ready days, rookies were unwelcome when they joined a big league team. As far as the veteran players were concerned, rookies were there to take somebody's job, so the older players banded together to protect each other. They had quickly found Jackson's Achilles' heel—his illiteracy and his ignorance of big-city ways.

Joe Jackson's illiteracy caused him to be taken by some as rude or stupid. Jackson, for example, was usually plainspoken, a practical necessity to avoid misunderstandings for anyone who must rely totally on the spoken word. Jackson was never able to convince people that just because he was unable to read and write he was not necessarily stupid. Though he may have lacked formal education, Jackson certainly had feelings, as his quick return home proved.

When Jackson got off the train back in Greenville, his parents were not happy to see him. They expected their son to make them proud in the big leagues. Jackson's mother wired Connie Mack that her son had come home because of illness in the family. Threatening to have Jackson banned from professional baseball, Mack ordered Tommy Stouch to escort the reluctant rookie back to Philadelphia again.

The Philadelphia sportswriters now began to criticize the young ballplayer. They decided that he could not take the pressure of the big leagues. They pointed out that the Athletics were about to play a pair of doubleheaders against the best team in the American League, the Detroit Tigers, and their new superstar, Ty Cobb. Perhaps, they suggested, Shoeless Joe was afraid to challenge Cobb.

Back in the lineup after a nine-day absence, Jackson played poorly. Another new star, who was the same age as Jackson, was pitching his first full season for the last-place Washington Senators. Walter Johnson, who would be re-

garded by many as the greatest pitcher in baseball history, held Jackson hitless in four trips.
Shoeless Joe went without a hit in another game
and then, suddenly, he was gone again. He had
packed his suitcase and gone home to Greenville
before the season ended. This time Connie Mack
did not try to bring him back.

Although Jackson's taste of big league life
had been a bitter one, he still believed that his
baseball skills would find him a job somewhere.
If the Philadelphia Athletics did not want him,
someone else would. He could always make a
living playing on mill teams and doing odd jobs.

*Connie Mack, owner
and manager of the
Philadelphia Athletics,
appreciated Jackson's
talent and worked hard
to build the youngster's
self-confidence. Mack's
efforts eventually
paid off, but his own
ballclub never reaped
the benefits.*

But Mack was not quite ready to give up on Jackson. The owner decided to let Jackson play another season in a southern minor league, hoping that he would mature.

Mack assigned Jackson's contract to Savannah, a comfortable Georgia city, in the South Atlantic (Sally) League. Whatever else the move to Savannah may have done for Jackson, it changed his life in one very important aspect: it got him a wife, 15-year-old Katherine Wynn. (At that time, especially in rural communities, it was not unusual for women to be married at an early age.) On July 19, Jackson's name was copied into the marriage register, and he and Katherine, whom everyone called Katie, began a life together that lasted until Jackson's death 47 years later.

No doubt the presence of an understanding person in his life helped Jackson, and he again led a league in batting, topping the Sally League with an impressive .358 before reporting back to Philadelphia at the tail end of the 1909 season. Once more, Jackson was the target of envious teammates and cynical sportswriters. And once more, he was miserable. Years later he told an interviewer, "Mr. Mack was a nice man and he was very patient and kind to me. But the others made me feel as poorly as a man can ever get to be."

Once, while the team was assembled on a train platform, Jackson noticed a row of large milk cans. Each had a red tag on which was written the name of the depot where it would be dropped off. As Mack walked by, Jackson pointed to the row of containers. "Mr. Mack, I wish you'd put a tag on me that said 'Greenville' and have the trainman just drop me off at home."

After the 1909 season, Mack was preparing to take his Athletics on a postseason cross-country tour that featured a series of games against an all-star team. Mack wanted to take Jackson along, feeling it would help him to gain poise. Walter Johnson was one of the pitchers for the other team, and most of the players on both teams, like Jackson, were still young. They included Jackson's teammates Home Run Baker and Eddie Collins, as well as Chief Meyers, the great Native American catcher who was breaking in with the New York Giants. But Jackson had no interest in a two-month tour when Katie and home cooking waited for him back in South Carolina.

In 1910, Mack sent Jackson to play for the Southern League's New Orleans team. Once again, Jackson led the league in batting with a .354 average, proof that he was ready for the major leagues. Mack, however, had concluded that Jackson simply would not shine in Philadelphia. To give the headstrong southerner a fresh start, he traded him to Cleveland. The Cleveland owner, Charles Somers, was a close friend of Mack's, and he was having a hard time keeping the fans interested in his team now that his star player, Napoleon Lajoie, was fading. Somers needed a player of Joe Jackson's promise to rebuild the franchise.

Jackson fulfilled the role brilliantly, hitting .387 for Cleveland in the final 20 games of 1910. Connie Mack had been right: having Jackson play in small and medium-sized cities had given him the chance to learn how to adjust to life away from home. Jackson now had more confidence in himself both on the field and off. He was finally ready to begin a career in the major leagues.

4

THE CLEVELAND YEARS

Elegantly if somewhat bizarrely shod, Jackson loosens up his arm before a game against the New York Highlanders. Despite his image as a "shoeless" country bumpkin, Jackson was a stylish dresser who enjoyed the material comforts his baseball income provided.

In 1911 Jackson was ready for big-time baseball, and Cleveland was ready for him. Cleveland had been a National League franchise before becoming one of the original teams that formed the American League in 1901. But in neither league had the ballclub ever won a pennant. Itching for glory, Jackson's new teammates knew that they needed him in order to succeed. They warned him that word was out around the league that Shoeless Joe could not take taunts. As soon as the season started, it became obvious that Jackson was a target every time he stepped into the batter's box. Having been prepared for this, he learned to turn it to his advantage. He would duck the pitches thrown at his head and wait until the pitcher, behind in the count, had to throw one over the plate—Jackson would jump on that pitch and line it for a base hit.

Jackson started where he had left off at the end of the previous season. His average stayed between .380 and .390 until midseason. Then, when most hitters begin to tail off, he went on a batting splurge that raised his average over

29

.400. At that point a head-to-head competition with Ty Cobb began in earnest. Cobb was working on his fifth straight American League batting championship, but he had never cracked the .400 mark. Now that he had someone pushing him, Cobb raised his game to new heights. His title-winning .420 average was the highest that he would ever achieve in his 24 seasons in the major leagues. Jackson's .408 average was only good enough for second place. It is characteristic of Jackson's career that he is the only rookie to ever hit over .400 and the only American Leaguer to top that mark and not win a batting championship.

Jackson's heroics could only elevate the Cleveland club to third place, but his brilliant season won over the fans and the writers. Their admiration for his hitting was matched by genuine sympathy: it was hard to imagine that a man could hit .408 and not even win the batting title. Legends about Jackson's prowess with the bat began to grow. The story circulated that his eyes were so sharp that he could see the trademark on a fastball as it roared toward the plate.

Despite Jackson's growing self-assurance on the ballfield and his popularity with the fans, his illiteracy continued to complicate his life. The most influential baseball writer during Jackson's career, Hugh Fullerton, Jr., was a relentless critic. Fullerton never tired of insisting that Jackson's success would encourage the nation's youth to scorn schoolwork: why should they study when Joe Jackson showed them it was possible to be a star even when you could not read your own press clippings?

The practical problems of life were even more difficult. Jackson could rely on his wife to read things for him at home—his baseball contracts, for example. When he was on the road, however, he could not even read a menu. Striving to cover up his illiteracy, he would order last in a restaurant, pretending to study the menu. Then he would say, "That sounds good, I'll have the same." If a document had to be signed, Jackson would say, "Leave it and come back tomorrow after I've had a chance to sleep on it."

From 1912 to 1914, Jackson batted .395, .373, and .338. But Cobb appeared to own the batting title, hitting .410, .390, and .368 for the

Before a 1912 game in Cleveland, Jackson talks hitting with two of the all-time greats, Detroit's Ty Cobb (left) and Wahoo Sam Crawford. Despite Jackson's brilliance as a hitter, he could never beat out the fiercely competitive Cobb for the batting title.

same three years. Still, it was a happy time in Jackson's life, and he would probably have been content to remain with Cleveland for his entire career. Joe and Katie lived comfortably during the season in a residential hotel, and they enjoyed spending the money that now came Jackson's way. Many of the "shoeless" star's fans would have been surprised if they could have seen the inside of his closet, which contained dozens of pairs of shoes in all styles.

Between seasons, Jackson went on the vaudeville circuit to cash in on his celebrity. This was a typical sideline for well-known ballplayers, requiring only a minimum of stage presence. Jackson would appear before the audience, swing Black Betsy across the footlights a few times, and answer some questions put to him by a female assistant.

The Jacksons spent much of the vaudeville earnings on a new car. This purchase led to a fateful incident in 1915 that convinced the Indians that it was time to cash in on their investment in Jackson before it was too late. One night midway in the season, Joe and Katie were out in their car when the engine suddenly stalled. Jackson lifted the hood and, standing on the running board, told Katie to get behind the wheel. While she put the car in gear and got it rolling, Joe leaned over the engine and tried to fix the problem. A passing wagon knocked him off the running board, and he was dragged 30 feet before Katie could stop the car.

Jackson's injuries kept him out of action for several weeks. Before he could get back in the lineup, Cleveland sold his contract to the Chicago White Sox for $65,000. This was a great deal of money in the eyes of Charles

Comiskey, the White Sox owner. Comiskey was spending freely and was assembling what might have been the greatest ballclub ever put together. The team would eventually self-destruct, largely because Comiskey could not grasp the idea that players who were bought and sold for large sums also expected to be paid well for their services. His stinginess when it came to paying salaries would come back to haunt him when eight of his players coldly sold out the 1919 World Series to gamblers.

5

COMING TO CHICAGO

Despite the warm welcome Jackson got when he and Katie drove over from Cleveland to Chicago, he did not play up to the fans' expectations. He had been batting .331 with the Indians, but in 46 games with the White Sox, he hit only .265. His .308 season average was the lowest of his career. However, he got his bearings in 1916 and almost carried the White Sox to a pennant while hitting .341, scoring 91 runs, and leading the league in total bases with 293. The White Sox finished close behind the Boston Red Sox, whose brilliant young left-handed pitcher, Babe Ruth, topped the league in ERA and won 23 games.

The White Sox' strength, in addition to Jackson and second baseman Eddie Collins, was their pitching. Eddie Cicotte (pronounced SEE-cot) and Claude "Lefty" Williams (both would likely have made the Baseball Hall of Fame had they stayed honest) combined with Red Faber (who did both) to form a strong mound corps. For Jackson, the presence of Williams, a native of Aurora, Missouri, was the

In the uniform of the Chicago White Sox, Jackson takes batting practice before a 1918 game. During his five full seasons with the Sox, Jackson was the team's best hitter, averaging .345.

35

First baseman Chick Gandil, who joined the White Sox in 1917, was a reliable clutch hitter and an excellent fielder. He also became one of the principal figures in the so-called Black Sox scandal of 1919.

prelude to disaster. The Williamses and the Jacksons became very good friends and remained so until their playing careers were cut short by the Black Sox scandal.

In 1917, the team that Charles Comiskey had so lavishly put together jelled and won the pennant with 100 victories. No White Sox team before or since has won as many games. Though Jackson himself had a subpar year, batting only .301, he had a more than adequate supporting cast. Chick Gandil, a smooth-fielding and smooth-talking first baseman, had been

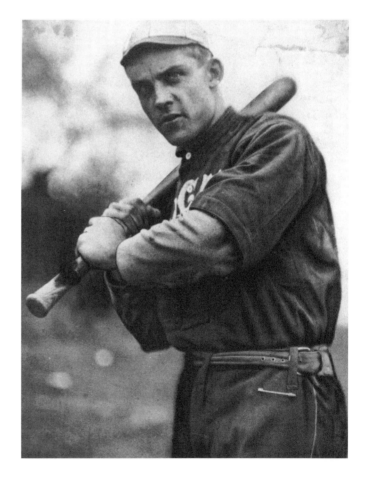

bought from Washington. Catcher Ray Schalk, third baseman Buck Weaver, and outfielder Happy Felsch were among the team's other stars.

In the 1917 World Series, the White Sox rolled over the National League champions, the New York Giants. Red Faber, a spitball pitcher, won three games for Chicago, and Cicotte won the other. Jackson had a good series, batting .307 and making several game-saving catches. The newly crowned world champions, however, were sidetracked by World War I before they could create a winning dynasty. In 1917 the United States had joined Britain, France, and Russia to fight Germany and Austria-Hungary. By 1918 the war's impact on baseball, as well as the nation's manpower and resources, was deeply felt.

When the government said "Work or Fight" to men of draft age, major league ballclubs were hard hit. Many ballplayers patriotically joined the armed forces. Ty Cobb, Christy Mathewson, and Grover Alexander were among the superstars who traded their baseball flannels for army uniforms. Some, with families to support, were deferred.

Various members of the White Sox reacted to the call to arms differently. Eddie Collins joined the Marines. Ray Schalk was enlisting in the army when the armistice was signed in 1918. Chick Gandil, however, the future ringleader of the Black Sox, and Swede Risberg found shipyard jobs in California. Happy Felsch ran a saloon in Milwaukee and somehow escaped the eye of his draft board. Eddie Cicotte, with a working farm, had a legitimate excuse to stay out of service. Lefty Williams, who was draft deferred, jumped the ballclub anyway to take a defense job.

Eddie Collins, a perennial .300 hitter, a deft second baseman, and a leading base stealer, was the White Sox' best player after Jackson. Untainted by the Black Sox scandal, Collins played 25 seasons in the major leagues and was elected to the Hall of Fame in 1939.

Chicago catcher Ray Schalk is tagged out at second base in the eighth inning of Game 3 of the 1917 World Series. The New York Giants won the game, 2–0, but the White Sox took the Series in six games.

Jackson and his wife were childless, but he supported his disabled brother, Davey, and his mother. Nonetheless, the Greenville draft board classifed Jackson as A-1 in the draft, making him eligible for induction. Jackson then did what many other players did: he found a job in a defense industry. Once again, he was singled out for more than his fair share of criticism. Charley Comiskey lashed out at him, saying that he was a coward and would not be welcome back on the team.

Perhaps significantly, in light of what was to come, Williams and Jackson ended up as teammates in the Bethlehem Steel League. The league was made up of teams from war plants

around the Delaware Basin, near Philadelphia. Most of the "workers" who formed the teams in the league were former big leaguers or minor league players.

Jackson again confounded his critics by being the drawing card of the league, whose games entertained thousands of wartime workers. Shoeless Joe was repeatedly in the lineup of extra Sunday games that raised money for the armed forces and local charities. Presumably he did his share of shipbuilding, and he and Lefty Williams rewarded their wartime employer with a championship. Jackson's bat and glove and Williams's arm won the final game of a defense industry "World Series."

The real 1918 World Series was played between the Red Sox and the Chicago Cubs. The Red Sox emerged triumphant, 4 games to 2, with Babe Ruth winning two games. Because of pressure from the War Department, the major leagues had shortened the season by a month and played the World Series right after Labor Day. Then, on November 11, 1918, the "war to end all wars" ceased. Charles Comiskey stopped criticizing his ballplayers and began to get ready for the fateful 1919 season.

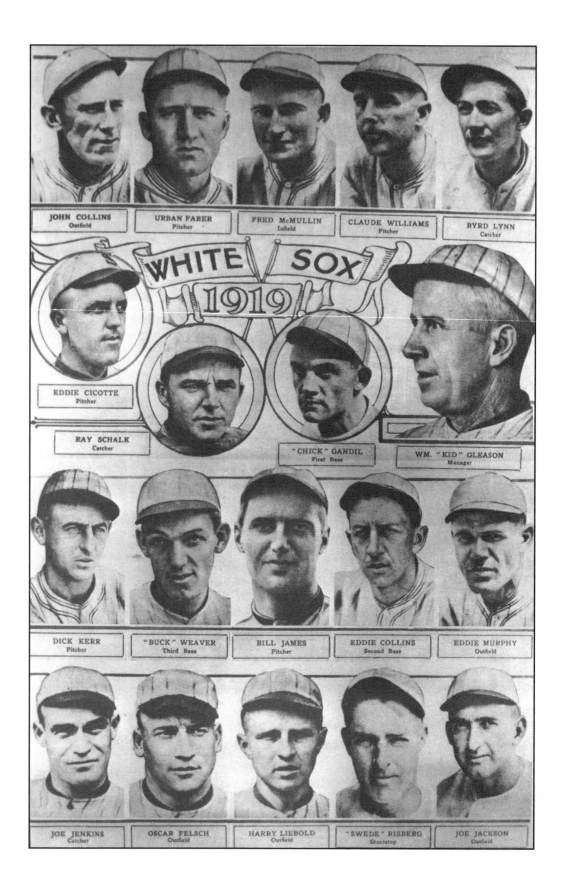

6

THE TEAM THAT COULDN'T LOSE

Ａs baseball got ready for the 1919 season, there were rumors that some big league players had fixed games in recent years. The Cubs' Hal Chase, a nimble first baseman and clever batter, drew suspicion wherever he went. Yet he was such a skillful player that some team always gave him another chance. John McGraw, the tough manager of the New York Giants, was certain his second baseman, Buck Herzog, had deliberately misplayed a number of ground balls during the 1917 World Series.

The public's penchant for betting on sports events has always created the possibility that players could be persuaded to cheat. In recent years players have been earning so much money that they would be foolish to risk their livelihood in return for payoffs from gamblers. This was not the case in Joe Jackson's time. Players had no pension plans and could be fired whenever a team's owner wished. Every player had a one-year contract and was obliged to play his entire career with the team that had first signed him. Thus, the players had very little leverage in bar-

A composite photo of the 1919 White Sox. Owner Charles Comiskey said of this team, "It's the best bunch of fighters I ever saw. With them, no game is lost until the last man is out."

41

gaining with owners. After a good year, a player could expect a modest raise; after a mediocre year, a pay cut was usually in order. Most baseball players felt that they were underpaid, and some lacked the character to resist temptation.

Although the war had ended, the major leagues played a shortened schedule in 1919, as they had the previous year. The White Sox outplayed their closest rivals, the Cleveland Indians, Joe Jackson's former team, and won the pennant by 3 ½ games. Chicago had a new manager, a hard-bitten veteran, Kid Gleason, who juggled the team's disruptive cliques into a winning ballclub.

Despite rumors that players had not tried their hardest in certain past games, no one thought it would be possible to rig a World Series. The Series was too important, and too many players would have to be involved. Never-

William "Kid" Gleason, a veteran of 22 seasons as a major league player, took over as manager of the White Sox in 1919. After guiding his talented players to a pennant, the hard-bitten Gleason was sickened and enraged by their poor play in the World Series.

theless, on the eve of the 1919 Fall Classic, baseball people and writers heard rumors that the Series had been tampered with. The fans, however, had total faith in their heroes.

The White Sox' opponents in the Series were the Cincinnati Reds. When big-time gamblers with heavy bankrolls poured into Cincinnati, where the Series was slated to begin, they offered odds that the White Sox would lose. Hugh Fullerton and other alert sportswriters were quick to notice. Admittedly, the Reds had posted the best record in baseball for the regular season. But the baseball experts believed that the American League was the tougher league by far, and they rated the White Sox one of the great teams of all time. Thus Chicago should have been the heavy favorite. Why were all the professional gamblers suddenly betting against them?

When the Reds surprised the experts by beating Eddie Cicotte in the opening game 9–1, Kid Gleason and his catcher, Ray Schalk, were puzzled and angry. Schalk said that Cicotte had constantly crossed him up by not throwing the pitches that Schalk had called for. Cicotte had led the league with 29 wins and allowed less than two runs a game. Yet the Reds had ripped his pitches at will. Gleason complained that the players had not followed his instructions about positioning themselves in the field. Even worse, some of them had seemed to loaf on fly balls or throw wildly. Comiskey, the miserly White Sox owner, hoped that his team had just had an off day. But the Sox proceeded to drop Game 2 the next day by a score of 4–2. Lefty Williams, the Chicago pitcher, mysteriously lost his control in the fourth inning, issuing three walks and being tagged for three runs.

During Game 2 of the 1919 World Series, Chick Gandil is called out while trying to steal second base. When Kid Gleason spotted Gandil cheerfully smoking a cigar after the White Sox' second straight loss, the manager pounced on the first baseman and tried to strangle him.

The teams rode the train to Chicago for Game 3. This time, Chicago pitcher Dickey Kerr, who was not in on the plot, shut out the Reds by a score of 3–0. Three of the players to be later accused of throwing the Series accounted for two of the White Sox' runs, as Chick Gandil doubled in the second inning to drive in Jackson and Felsch.

Eddie Cicotte had learned to hide his intentions better in his next start, allowing only five hits. However, he made two fielding errors in the fifth inning—on one play, he muffed a throw from Jackson—and gave the Reds two runs. Cincinnati's Jimmy Ring shut out the White Sox, and the Reds moved ahead 3 games to 1.

Lefty Williams repeated his dubious efforts in Game 5, won by the Reds, 5–0. Whether the

White Sox' failure to score once again was due to Reds pitcher Hod Eller is a matter of debate. Eller, second in strikeouts during the regular season, fanned six batters in a row at one point. The feat still ranks as a World Series record, though under the circumstances it will always be suspect.

When the Series shifted back to Cincinnati, Kerr again staved off a White Sox defeat in extra innings. The win brought the best-of-nine-games Series to 4-2. The next game that Cicotte pitched was a return to his true form, a 4–1 triumph. Later revelations suggested that the crooked players had not been paid all the money the gamblers had promised. They responded by playing their best.

By this time, the White Sox were close enough to pull out the Series. If Lefty Williams could only pitch up to form in Game 8, the Series would be tied, and perhaps Kerr could win the deciding game. Unfortunately, Kerr never got the chance.

In writing about the 1919 World Series in his memoir, *Baseball As I Have Known It,* veteran reporter Fred Lieb recounted his impressions of Game 8: "I happened to stop at the men's lavatory under the grandstand before I went to the press box. There were several men there whom I knew to be big time gamblers. They were worried that the White Sox would win after all. Then another gambler rushed in shouting, 'It's all set. The game will be over in the first inning.' "

Lieb watched from the press box as Lefty Williams threw almost every pitch right down the middle to the Reds batters. He was racked for five straight hits and four runs before Kid Gleason, knowing he had been betrayed, yanked the left-hander with only one out. The Reds coasted to a 10–5 "triumph." Joe Jackson had unleashed Black Betsy for a token swing, hitting a solo home run when the score was 5–0. The home run, along with his series-leading .375 average, would later be used by Jackson's supporters as an argument that he had played to win.

The best case that can be made for Joe Jackson is that he was betrayed by his friend and roommate, Lefty Williams. Supporters of this theory contend that the gamblers would not give the players the money they wanted unless Jackson, the team's best player, was part of the plot. Knowing how close Williams and Jackson were off the field, they took the pitcher's word that his buddy was in on the plan and never met with Jackson.

It is inconceivable, however, that Jackson did not know of Williams's plotting. They were roommates on the road and shared a room at the Sinton Hotel in Cincinnati when the Series opened there. Jackson was probably torn between his competitive drive and his friendship with Williams, plus the influence of the ringleader, Chick Gandil.

Although no one can be sure how often Jackson might have failed to bear down at the plate or purposely made a poor fielding play, an analysis of his .375 average raises some questions. When Eddie Cicotte hit the leadoff man with a pitch, signaling the gamblers that the White Sox intended to lose the opener, Jackson might well have taken his cue. He went hitless in four times at bat.

Perhaps sickened by the idea of losing on purpose, Jackson rapped out three hits in four at-bats in Game 2. Knowing that Dickey Kerr was outside the conspiracy, Jackson kept up his steady batting with a 3-for-3 day in Game 3.

In the next game, Jackson's intentions might have swung back to the losing side with Cicotte back on the mound: he had one hit in four at-bats. Then, probably accepting that Williams was set on losing, Jackson went hitless in Game 5. Dickey Kerr, the one honest starter, got Jackson's help in Game 6 when Black Betsy rapped out a pair of hits. When Eddie Cicotte suddenly bore down in the next game, Jackson chipped in with another 2-for-4 day. Finally, after Williams put the crucial game out of reach in the first inning, Jackson was left to his own devices. He had flied out his first time up, but then hit his home run and added another hit to go 2-for-5.

Jackson had 12 hits, a record for World Series play. However, in Cicotte's first two starts and Williams's second effort, Jackson had only one hit in 12 plate appearances. His overall .375 breaks down to .555 when he was presumably trying and .083 when there is reason to think that he was not. These figures would seem to damage the claim that he did his best in every game. Given his close association with Lefty Williams, it is not conceivable that he was just an innocent country boy who had no idea seven of his teammates were determined to make a lot of money by losing on purpose.

By Jackson's own account before the grand jury, after the series ended in Cincinnati, a drunken Lefty Williams offered Jackson a soiled envelope containing $5,000 in cash. It was Jackson's share, Williams said. When Jackson refused to take the money, Williams threw the envelope on Jackson's bed. The next day,

Jackson presumably attempted to give the money to the White Sox. He went to see Charles Comiskey but was headed off by the team's secretary, Harry Grabiner, who insisted that the owner was busy and could not be bothered. After waiting several hours, Jackson went home.

Jackson said he kept the cash in his house for several months until Katie insisted he put it in the bank for safety. Eventually, Jackson seems to have concluded that whether he wanted to keep the money or not, there was no one to whom he could give it back. For those who credit his claim that he was not part of the plot, it can be surmised that the money in the envelope was half of Lefty Williams's $10,000 bribe, the same payoff that Eddie Cicotte had collected at the start of the fixed series. In this view, Williams, who had brought Jackson's name into the plot without his friend's consent, was making amends.

Claude "Lefty" Williams, one of the main culprits in the plot to throw the 1919 World Series, was also Jackson's best friend on the White Sox. Because of his connection with Williams, Jackson was drawn into the conspiracy.

*Veteran pitcher Eddie
Cicotte, a 29-game winner
in 1919, accepted $10,000
to do less than his best
during the World Series.
A year later, he remorse-
fully told a grand jury,
"I've lived a thousand
years in the last twelve
months. I would not have
done that thing for a
million dollars."*

Eliot Asinof's account of the 1919 World
Series scandal, *Eight Men Out*, takes a harsher
view of Jackson. Asinof contends that Jackson
agreed to join the plot but then suffered a guilty
conscience. For this reason, he tried to sit out
the first game of the series, but Gleason ordered
him to play. Immediately after the Series was
over, Jackson went to Comiskey to tell him about
the plot, and Comiskey refused to talk to him.
Finally, according to Asinof, Jackson dictated a
letter to Comiskey, stating that the games had
not been played fairly and offering to tell all he
knew. Comiskey never bothered to reply.

7

BANNED FOR LIFE

As baseball resumed in 1920, Joe Jackson and his teammates did not discuss the previous season. They hoped that all the talk about the Series having been fixed would blow over, and the whole affair would be forgotten. For a while it seemed that their wishes might be realized, as the White Sox began to have a great season. They won game after game, as Lefty Williams mowed down batters and Jackson smashed blue darters all over the lot.

Soon enough, however, there were signs that the previous year's Series was going to haunt the team. Gamblers were emboldened by the piles of money that they had made in 1919 and instructed White Sox players to lose certain games. The odds on those games would then suddenly shift dramatically. These and other even more brazen tactics—especially with the highly suspect 1919 Series still a fresh memory—inevitably reached the ears of baseball reporters. They in turn talked to key figures in the baseball world as well as prominent citizens who loved the game.

Stories began to appear in the press, and pressure began to build for an investigation. A grand jury was convened to determine whether

Charles Comiskey, known as the Old Roman, was quick to suspend the Chicago players accused in the Black Sox scandal, but he himself bore part of the blame. Because of his insistence on paying rock-bottom salaries, his underpaid players were vulnerable to bribe offers.

players had been corrupted by gamblers. Detectives and reporters began to follow leads. When a newspaperman finally located the bitter ex-ballplayer Billy Maharg, who had helped fix the Series but had not been paid by the gamblers, the story broke onto the front pages.

Kid Gleason had been watching Eddie Cicotte all summer and sensed that he was about to break under the intense pressure. Gleason was right. When Comiskey summoned Cicotte to his office, the pitcher began confessing his involvement in throwing the Series even before he was asked a single question. Comiskey angrily shouted, "Don't tell me! Tell it to the grand jury!" Cicotte did just that, revealing the entire conspiracy.

Joe Jackson decided to call the judge presiding over the grand jury investigation the day after the story broke in the newspapers. The judge urged him to come and testify, and after learning that Cicotte had confessed, Jackson, too, took his turn before the grand jury. Jackson admitted to the jurors that he had agreed to go along with the plot, after being hounded repeatedly by Chick Gandil and Swede Risberg. Though he did not confess to having played poorly on purpose, he admitted that he was disappointed with his performance. Jackson also claimed that he had been betrayed by Gandil and Risberg, who had promised him $20,000 and then offered him only $5,000. After his testimony, Jackson appeared to feel that he had cleared himself. "I got a big load off my chest!" he told the court officers who escorted him out.

When the grand jury concluded its investigation, indictments were issued against eight

White Sox ballplayers for conspiring to fix the 1919 World Series. The accused players were Chick Gandil, Happy Felsch, Buck Weaver, Swede Risberg, Fred McMullin (a utility infielder), Eddie Cicotte, Lefty Williams, and—most shocking to the fans—Joe Jackson.

However, by the time the players were actually brought into a court of law 10 months later, Jackson's confession and the sworn admissions of the others had "disappeared" from the files. A new district attorney had been elected, and he could not present a strong case without the documents. The players, guided by defense lawyers who had been on the first district attorney's staff when the indictments were handed down, had by now changed their stories. After all the testimony was heard, the jury rendered a verdict of not guilty. The jurors appeared to take a civic pride in preserving the baseball careers of the White Sox players.

Whether Charles Comiskey would have welcomed the acquitted players back will never be

Judge Kenesaw Mountain Landis (rear, left), the first commissioner of baseball, presides over a 1921 hearing into the Black Sox scandal. Landis later decreed that eight Chicago players including Swede Risberg and Chick Gandil (rear, center) be banned for life from professional baseball.

known. The baseball owners, frightened that the scandal would ruin the game and wipe out their investments, hired baseball's first commissioner, Kenesaw Mountain Landis. Landis was a well-known federal judge with a reputation for fearless, if erratic, justice. The owners granted him total power over the conduct of baseball. Landis quickly dashed any hope that Joe Jackson and the other acquitted Black Sox had of resuming their careers.

The commissioner sneered at the jury's decision and rendered his own judgment: "Regardless of the verdict of juries, no player that throws a ball game, no player that undertakes or promises to throw a ball game, no player that sits in conference with a bunch of crooked players and gamblers where the ways and means of throwing a game are discussed and does not promptly tell his club about it, will ever play professional baseball."

Landis's verdict was final, and there was no possibility of appeal. He also made it clear that any players who took part in exhibition games with the banned Black Sox would also be expelled from the game.

Jackson made a number of attempts to play in the minor leagues under assumed names. Sometimes he called himself Johnson, and in a Hackensack, New Jersey, game he was listed on the program as Joseph. But his talent always gave him away. The best that he ever did as an undercover player was to last 35 games in an outlaw league in Louisiana. Teaming up with Eddie Cicotte and Swede Risberg, he batted .500 as his club dominated the competition.

Ultimately Jackson had to look elsewhere for his livelihood. After leaving Chicago, he and

Shoeless Joe Jackson in 1922, when he was trying to earn a living as a semipro player. Though he appeared under assumed names, his immense talent quickly betrayed his true identity.

Katie had settled in Savannah, Georgia, where he opened a dry-cleaning business. In 1929 the Jacksons moved back to Greenville. There he opened a second dry-cleaning business and played semipro ball in the summer. Though they had no children of their own, Joe and Katie helped to raise two of Joe's nephews.

Essentially, Jackson settled into an obscure but honorable life. In Greenville he was a favorite of the local boys, who would gather on his front porch and listen to his advice on the art of playing baseball and the importance of a man's honor. He continued to maintain his innocence of having thrown the 1919 World Series, and eventually a movement was begun to clear his name. In 1951 he was scheduled to make an appearance on national television, then in its infancy. In addition to presenting his side of the Black Sox scandal, he was eager to let people know that he had not been a failure after he left

When he posed for this 1935 photograph, Jackson was living quietly and comfortably in his old hometown. After his death in 1951, his admirers began a campaign to clear his name and secure his election to the Baseball Hall of Fame.

baseball. He was especially annoyed that a magazine writer had described him as "pressing pants for a living." By this time he owned a chain of dry-cleaning establishments and was a prosperous small-town businessman. Only several weeks before he was to go on the air, however, Jackson died of a heart attack. The date was December 5, 1951, and Jackson was 63 years old.

Despite Jackson's inability to plead his own case before the nation's baseball fans, the movement to clear his name continued to grow. By the 1990s, a number of prominent journalists were involved in the campaign to secure Jackson's admission into the Hall of Fame. Judged by his statistics alone, there is no question that he belongs in Cooperstown. Over the course of 13 big league seasons, Jackson batted .356, the third-highest average in baseball history: only Ty Cobb (.367) and Rogers Hornsby (.358) stand above him on the all-time list. If Jackson's supporters can convince the baseball world that he was truly a wronged man, he may be enshrined alongside other honorable members of the great 1919 White Sox team: Red Faber, Ray Schalk, Eddie Collins, and owner Charles Comiskey. Until that issue is decided, the legacy of Shoeless Joe Jackson will continue to fascinate and puzzle those who cherish the game of baseball.

CHRONOLOGY

1887	Born Joseph Jefferson Jackson in Pickens County, South Carolina, on July 16
1893	Moves with family to Brandon Mill
1901	Begins to play ball on Brandon Mill team
1906	Begins his semipro career with the Greenville Near Leaguers
1908	Enters professional baseball with Greenville in the Carolina Association and leads league in batting with a .346 average; marries Katherine Wynn; makes major league debut with Philadelphia Athletics
1910	Traded to Cleveland after playing two years in the minor leagues; hits .387 over final 20 games of season
1911	Bats .408 during his first full major league season, highest batting average ever by a rookie
1912	Bats .395 and leads American League in triples
1913	Leads American League with 197 hits and .551 slugging average
1915	Traded to Chicago White Sox
1917	Jackson bats .307 and stars in the field, leading White Sox to victory over New York Giants in the World Series
1918	Takes defense job during World War I
1919	Bats .351 during regular season; posts .375 average in World Series as White Sox lose to Cincinnati Reds
1920	Bats .385 during regular season and leads league in triples for third time; suspended after allegations that White Sox threw the 1919 World Series
1921	Chicago jury acquits Jackson of helping to fix the 1919 World Series; Judge Kenesaw Mountain Landis, first commissioner of baseball, bans Jackson and seven other Chicago players from organized base-ball for life
1922	Jackson moves to Savannah, Georgia, and opens dry-cleaning business
1929	Returns home to Greenville, South Carolina, where he lives quietly as a businessman and plays semipro ball
1951	Dies in Greenville on December 5

York Times.

WEDNESDAY, SEPTEMBER 29, 1920 TWO CENTS | In Greater New York | THREE CENTS Within 200 Miles | FOUR CENTS Elsewhere

EIGHT WHITE SOX PLAYERS ARE INDICTED ON CHARGE OF FIXING 1919 WORLD SERIES; CICOTTE GOT $10,000 AND JACKSON $5,000

Yankee Owners Give Praise to Comiskey And Offer Him Use of Their Whole Team

Following the announcement from Chicago yesterday that Owner Charles A. Comiskey had suspended two star pitchers, two regular infielders, his two leading outfielders and one utility player, Colonels Jacob Ruppert and T. L. Huston, owners of the New York Club, put at Comiskey's disposal the entire New York American League Club.

It is not likely, however, that the offer will be accepted. The reason advanced for the unusual offer is that such a grave and unforeseen emergency requires an unusual remedy. An American League rule prevents the transfer of a player from one club to another after July 1 without the asking of waivers, which would give any club in the league an opportunity to get the player. This is the technicality referred to in the message.

The telegram from the Yankee owners to Comiskey read as follows:
Mr. Charles A. Comiskey, Chicago, Ill.:

Your action in suspending players under suspicion, although it wrecks your entire organization and perhaps your cherished lifework, not only challenges our admiration but excites our sympathy and demands our practical assistance. You are making a terrible sacrifice to preserve the integrity of the game. So grave and unforseen an emergency requires unusual remedies.

Therefore, in order that you may play out your schedule and, if necessary the world's series, our entire club is placed at your disposal. We are confident that Cleveland sportsmanship will not permit you to lose by default and will welcome the arrangement. We are equally certain that any technicality in carrying it out can be readily overcome by action on the part of the National Commission.

(Signed) JACOB RUPPERT,
T. L. HUSTON.

COMISKEY SUSPENDS THEM

Promises to Run Them Out of Baseball if Found Guilty

TWO OF PLAYERS CONFESS

Cicotte and Jackson Tell of Their Work in Throwing Games to Cincinnati.

BOTH ARE HELD IN CUSTODY

Prosecutor Says More Players Will Be Indicted and Gamblers Brought to Task.

MAJOR LEAGUE STATISTICS

PHILADELPHIA ATHLETICS, CLEVELAND INDIANS, CHICAGO WHITE SOX

YEAR	TEAM	G	AB	R	H	2B	3B	HR	RBI	BA	SB
1908	PHI A	5	23	0	3	0	0	0	3	.130	0
1909		5	17	3	5	0	0	0	3	.294	0
1910	CLE A	20	75	15	29	2	5	1	11	.387	4
1911		147	571	126	233	45	19	7	83	.408	41
1912		152	572	121	226	44	26	3	90	.395	35
1913		148	528	109	197	39	17	7	71	.373	26
1914		122	453	61	153	22	13	3	53	.338	22
1915	2 Teams	CLE A (82G - .331)			CHI A (46G - .265)						
	total	128	461	63	142	20	14	5	81	.308	16
1916	CHI A	155	592	91	202	40	21	3	78	.341	24
1917		146	538	91	162	20	17	5	75	.301	13
1918		17	65	9	23	2	2	1	20	.354	3
1919		139	516	79	181	31	14	7	96	.351	9
1920		146	570	105	218	42	20	12	121	.382	9
Totals		1330	4981	873	1774	307	168	54	785	.356	202
World Series											
1917	CHI A	6	23	1	3	1	0	0	2	.125	1
1919	CHI A	8	32	5	12	3	0	1	6	.375	0
Totals		14	55	6	15	4	0	1	8	.250	1

FURTHER READING

Asinof, Eliot. *Eight Men Out: The Black Sox and the 1919 World Series.* New York: Henry Holt, 1987.

Brown, Warren. *The Chicago White Sox.* New York: Putnam, 1952.

Dawidoff, Nicholas. "Too Good to Be Left Out." *Sports Illustrated*, June 12, 1989.

Farrell, James T. *My Baseball Diary.* New York: A. S. Barnes, 1957.

Frommer, Harvey. *Shoeless Joe and Ragtime Baseball.* Dallas: Taylor, 1992.

Gropman, Donald. *Say It Ain't So, Joe!: The True Story of Shoeless Joe Jackson.* New York: Carol Publishing Group, 1992.

Holtzman, Jerome. *No Cheering in the Press Box.* New York: Holt, Rinehart & Winston, 1974.

Jackson, Joe, as told to Furman Bisher. "This Is the Truth." *Sport*, October 1949.

Lieb, Frederick. *Baseball As I Have Known It.* New York: Coward, 1977.

Luhrs, Victor. *The Great Baseball Mystery—The 1919 World Series.* New York: A. S. Barnes, 1966.

Rice, Grantland. *The Tumult and the Shouting.* New York: Barnes, 1954.

Ritter, Lawrence. *The Glory of Their Times.* New York: Macmillan, 1966.

Sheed, Wilfrid. "One Man Out . . . Too Long." *GQ*, August 1990.

INDEX

TURE CREDITS

/Wide World Photos: p. 56; The Bettmann Archive: pp. 22, 28, 34, 53; Courtesy George Brace: p. 40; Chicago torical Society: pp. 2, 44; National Baseball Library, Cooperstown, NY: pp. 8, 20, 31, 36, 37, 42, 48, 49, 50, 55, South Caroliniana Library, University of South Carolina, Columbia: p. 14; Courtesy Jack Torciello/P.O. Box)8, Maplewood, NJ 07040: p. 18; UPI/Bettmann: pp. 12, 38.

JACK KAVANAGH, a freelance writer of sports stories, began writing about sports as a high school correspondent for the *Brooklyn Eagle* in the 1930s. He has been a contributing editor to *Sports History,* and his writing has appeared in various magazines, including *Sports Heritage, Vine Line,* and *Diversions.* His work is included in *The Ball Players, Total Baseball,* and other baseball anthologies. Mr. Kavanagh lives in North Kingston, Rhode Island.

JIM MURRAY, veteran sports columnist of the *Los Angeles Times,* is one of America's most acclaimed writers. He has been named "America's Best Sportswriter" by the National Association of Sportscasters and Sportswriters 14 times, was awarded the Red Smith Award, and was twice winner of the National Headliner Award. In addition, he was awarded the J. G. Taylor Spink Award in 1987 for "meritorious contributions to baseball writing." With this award came his 1988 induction into the National Baseball Hall of Fame in Cooperstown, New York. In 1990, Jim Murray was awarded the Pulitzer Prize for Commentary.

EARL WEAVER is the winningest manager in the Baltimore Orioles' history by a wide margin. He compiled 1,480 victories in his 17 years at the helm. After managing eight different minor league teams, he was given the chance to lead the Orioles in 1968. Under his leadership the Orioles finished lower than second place in the American League East only four times in 17 years. One of only 12 managers in big league history to have managed in four or more World Series, Earl was named Manager of the Year in 1979. The popular Weaver had his number 5 retired in 1982, joining Brooks Robinson, Frank Robinson, and Jim Palmer, whose numbers were retired previously. Earl Weaver continues his association with the professional baseball scene by writing, broadcasting, and coaching.